GEN'L FITZ JOHN PORTER'S

REPLY

TO

HON. Z. CHANDLER'S

SPEECH

IN THE U. S. SENATE, FEB. 21, 1870.

MORRISTOWN, N. J.
1870.

MORRISTOWN, N. J., *March*, 1870.

HON. Z. CHANDLER, *U. S. Senate:*

SIR—You introduced a resolution in the Senate of the United States, on the twenty-first February, "Requesting the President to communicate to the Senate, if not inconsistent with the public interests, any recent correspondence in his possession in relation to the case of Fitz John Porter."

On the occasion of offering the resolution you delivered a speech which has gone into the public debates and been published, and which will ever remain on the record as the expression of the opinion of a Senator of the United States, not only on the impropriety and injustice of according to me a re-hearing—but on the justice of my sentence, even in the light of the new facts which I propose to bring before any tribunal the President may appoint to re-hear the case.

Though you withdrew your resolution immediately after making your speech, the latter remains unanswered except by the generous words of the Hon. Henry Wilson, the chairman of the senate committee of military affairs during the whole war and since, who declared that he adhered to his formerly expressed opinion, that my case was, under the new evidence brought to light, a proper one to be re-heard. Indeed the withdrawal of your resolution was more prejudicial to me than the original offering of it; for if not withdrawn, the correspondence called for would have shown in a great measure the truth, and my title to a re-hearing.

It is a noble and a senatorial office, "to vindicate the truth of history," and you assured the Senate and the country that that was the object of your speech.

May I not ask, that you will read this, my letter to you, which is intended to show that you fell into grave errors in your endeavor to do justice to history. May I not also ask—as your inculpation of me—while I was appealing for a re-hearing of my case on new evidence, was presented for the public consideration in a speech from your seat in the Senate, and is thus preserved for ever in the printed debates—that you will, by some means familiar to you as a Senator, secure to me, the accused in that speech, the presentation and preservation of my defence and answer, in as advantageous a manner and in as desirable a form. This will vindicate the truth of history in the only way that it can be vindicated with justice to me—the accused.

I pray you to do me this justice.

In your speech you say that Mr. Lincoln, Mr. Stanton, and Gen. Wadsworth, who knew the facts, are now dead. They could not know them. They were not the witnesses. They could only know or believe what was told them. But if you mean that I have waited their death to make my appeal, you are greatly in error. I have made it from the first hour of the verdict, with constant urgency and all the force I could exert; and I have the proof that Mr. Lincoln, within a short period of his death, promised to re-open the case if new evidence was produced, and said—what some of the ablest and truest friends of his administration now say, among them some of your brother senators—that, in such case, a rehearing was not only just to me but due to the honor of the army.

I have also the further proof that Mr. Lincoln said that he had entertained a very high opinion of my bravery and fidelity, but had been obliged in this particular case, to form his opinion and base his action on the Judge-Advocate General's review, as in the multitude of his cares he had not been able to make a personal investigation.

I have also had very gratifying evidence, *since the trial*, of Gen. Wadsworth's friendship and confidence. You relate the opinion he expressed to you of the great and decisive result of the battle of Malvern. You will pardon me for asking you to remember also in what terms the commanding general assigned to me the chief merit of that great day.

I need not go into that half of your speech which is a commendation of General Pope. It would draw me from the proper line of my own defence. Much of what you say of him, I am not interested to deny. If he was put at the head of an army to rescue McClellan by the means you suggest—by "fooling correspondents," "fooling the country," and "fooling the rebels" with stories of his great force, I need not deny that he was the man for *that* part, although he did *not* " fool the rebels" (as he admits), whatever success in that business he had with others; and I may think it was somewhat in excess of any useful demand the government had on his pecnliar gift, to practice as he did on the good nature of Mr. Lincoln, and attempt to fool *him* with despatches of " great victories," of " driving the enemy from the field," " making great captures," &c., &c. But that is his affair, not mine. I think you are much in error about it. But I prefer to leave it so, and go on to my own business.

Stripped of all accessories by which they have been covered I present the charges on which I was arraigned, and my claims for a re-hearing.

The first accusation against me is that I disobeyed an order of Gen. Pope received at Warrenton Junction about 10 at night August 27, '62, directing me to march my command at 1 o'clock in the morning to Bristoe station, tēn miles distant, so as to be there by daylight. You have added to this charge that Hooker was out of ammunition, and *might* have been destroyed by not getting it from me.

The disobedience claimed consists in not marching till 3 o'clock in the morning—a delay of two hours.

I shall prove—when I get a re-hearing—that I put off starting—two hours only of night—by the urgent advice of the generals of division. Their reasons were the following:

That my command had reached Warrenton Junction at a late hour, without food, and very much fatigued by a long and difficult march, the last of thirteen days and nights of marching and broken rest; that the night was pitch dark, the road was bad and blocked up with wagon trains in considerable confusion:

That the spirit and purpose of the order would be best carried out by delaying the march till *daybreak*, because the troops would have their night's rest, and would make the march with more rapidity and fewer delays, and reach their destination in condition for immediate action; and,

That as we were informed " the enemy was then retiring" from before Gen. Pope, the necessity was not pressing, and as my command would be required to aid in "driving him from Manassas and clearing the country between that and Gainesville" the troops already worn out and needing rest and sleep, if required to renew the march at an earlier hour than day-break, would be disabled for the service several miles beyond Bristoe.

I shall prove that, though appreciating the soundness of their reasons, I was decidedly of the opinion that "the order should be obeyed;" that "he who gave the order knew whether the necessities of the case should warrant the exertions that had to be made to comply with it," and that I yielded to the advice of my Generals only after being assured that the bearer of the order had been delayed by the darkness of the night and the blocked condition of the road.

I shall prove that the result showed that literal compliance with the order was impracticable, that no time was lost by the delay, but the march made all the quicker for it; and that I arrived as soon as other troops, commanded by as true soldiers as ever breathed, coming a shorter distance and under as urgent orders.

I shall prove that when I did arrive, there was and had been nothing for me to do, and that I remained at Bristoe all that day, under injunctions from Gen. Pope, twice repeated through the day, "to remain at Bristoe, when wanted you will be sent for."

I shall prove also, that I knew nothing about Hooker wanting ammunition, and that he did not want any, *and did not take any when it reached him.*

In brief:—I shall prove this charge of Pope's not only false, but frivolous and only suggested as a make weight to the far more serious accusations arising from the transactions of the next day.

New proof is ready on all these points.

The events of the 27th and 28th of August being thus briefly given and my conduct on those days narrated, I am brought to the events of the 29th.

On the morning of that day the following order—known as the "joint order" was issued by Gen. Pope.—

HEADQUARTERS ARMY OF VIRGINIA,
CENTREVILLE, August 29, 1862.

Generals McDowell and Porter.

"You will please move forward with your joint commands toward Gainesville. I sent General Porter written orders to that effect an hour and a half ago. Heintzelman, Sigel and Reno are moving on Warrenton turnpike, and must now be not far from Gainesville. I desire that as soon as communication is established between this force and your own, the whole command shall halt. It may be necessary to fall back behind Bull Run, at Centreville to-night. I presume it will be so on account of our supplies.

"I have sent no orders of any description to Ricketts, and none to interfere in any way with the movements of McDowell's troops, except what I sent by his aide-de camp last night, which were to hold his position on the Warrenton pike until the troops from here should fall on the enemy's flank and rear. I do not even know Rickett's position, as I have not been able to find out where General McDowell was until a late hour this morning. General Mc Dowell will take immediate steps to communicate with General Ricketts and instruct him to join the other divisions of his corps as soon as practicable.

"*If any considerable advantages are to be gained by departing from this order, it will not be strictly carried out.* One thing must be held in view, that the troops must occupy a position from which they can reach Bull Run to-night or by morning.

"The indications are that the whole force of the enemy is moving in this direction at a pace that will bring them here by to-morrow night or the next day.

"My own headquarters will for the present be with Heintzelman's corps, or at this place.

"JOHN POPE, Major-General Commanding."

The accusation is that I disobeyed this order. You charge "inaction" under it.

The record shows it to have been a substitute for a previous order from Gen. Pope to me; that when I received it I was moving along the Manassas road and upon Gainesville, having my own corps (less than 11,000) and King's division of McDowell's corps and that my purpose was to prevent the junction of Longstreet with Jackson—that event having been made imminent by the withdrawal of the troops of Ricketts and King from the road the enemy would have to traverse.

The "joint order" was instigated principally by a note from me to Gen. Pope, asking for written orders to take the place of contradictory verbal orders, which I had received from him, and giving him information I had obtained from various sources.

The terms of the "joint order" show that Gen. Pope intended to form his army in front of or near Gainesville, in order that he might be prepared to fall back "behind Bull Run that night or next morning"; that McDowell and myself were merely ordered to advance far enough to communicate with the rest of the army and then halt, and on no account to advance so far that we could not fall back to Bull Run by morning at least, or as the order says, "the troops must occupy a position from which they can reach Bull Run to-night or by morning." It contemplated no offensive combat, beyond that necessary to effect the commnnication with the rest of the army.

The record shows that Pope's statement in the "joint order" that the troops under Heintzleman, Sigel and Reno, were "moving on Warrenton turnpike and must now be not far from Gainesville," was wrong. They were all near Groveton, four miles distant from Gainesville, and were arrested by Jackson's troops.

About noon Gen. McDowell appeared, and showing me the "joint order," took command. Prior to its receipt, *I had been moving toward Gainesville, and, at the time of its receipt, had come in contact with the enemy, and was coming into position*, when McDowell appeared—the rear of my column being near the junction of the Manassas and Sudley Spring roads.

Gen. McDowell testified that "When the 'joint order' reached us we were doing what that joint order directed us to do. That joint order found the troops in the position it directed them to be." It seems clear, therefore, that up to noon, 29th, according to Gen. McDowell, both he and I, were faithfully doing as we had been directed, and that our *action*, (not "*in*-action") fulfilled Gen. Pope's order to us jointly.

I had ample reason to believe, then (noon 29th) that Longstreet's forces *had formed their junction* with Jackson. I submitted proof upon my trial, to sustain an assertion so vitally important to me. My assertion was contradicted, my proof was disbelieved, and the court coinciding with Pope's "assertion," McDowell's "belief," and Judge Advocate Holt's "assumption" of Longstreet's force being far distant from me, held me responsible and guilty.

When I shall show, by Longstreet's own testimony, how cruel a wrong this mass of bold assertion, wrong belief, and prejudiced assumption has done me, what just man can gainsay *my right to be heard?*

The record shows that after discussion of the injunctions in the "joint order" and in exercise of the discretion given in it—"that if any considerable advantages are to be gained by departing from this order, it will not be strictly carried out"—Gen. McDowell, still in command, decided to withdraw from my column his portion of the troops (over one-half) and gave me a verbal order, about which there is a dispute. He testifies the question was not one of "advance," and that he ordered me "to *post* my troops in to the right of the head of the "column of *where I then was*," "*to put my troops in there.*"

The record further shows that two officers testify that they heard Gen. McDowell say to me when he first joined me at the head of the column and I had come in contact with the enemy, "Porter you are too far *out*; this is no place to fight a battle."

I have asserted and ever shall assert, that Gen. McDowell's order to me was "to remain where I then was, while he would "place King's division on my right and form the connection "enjoined in the 'joint order.'" This order to me and statement of what he himself was about to do, were intended to accomplish a purpose very much desired by Gen. McDowell. The assignment of King to me annoyed him, and he had previously obtained from me, while at Manassas, a promise that I would place King on my right in the new line about to be formed, so that connecting with Reynolds (then at Groveton) his (McDowell's) troops would be together and at the proper time, he might reclaim King. Gen. McDowell by the above order and statement undertook to discharge me from my promise and to do himself what he desired—have King with him.

An immediate examination by us of the country towards Groveton, showed the impracticability of doing *directly* what he desired, "placing King on my right and thus forming connection with the troops near Groveton"—and Gen. McDowell left me without further instruction, but with the understanding that he would, by going *around* behind the woods separating us from Groveton, take King and uniting Ricketts with him, join his command (Reynolds and Sigel) then at Groveton.

While returning to my command, seeing the enemy forming in our front, I determined to attack at once with our combined forces and sent my chief of staff to King's division to prevent its withdrawal, resuming at the same time the deployment of my troops, arrested by McDowell.

My chief of staff soon returned bringing from Gen. McDowell the message for me "to remain where I was, and if compelled "to fall back to do so on his left." He had found McDowell with King's division. I could then regard this message only as the renewal of McDowell's first injunction, not now, in the face of a superior force, to be disregarded—and at once recalled my troops to the position they held when he left me. From that time till the receipt of an order dated 4:30 P. M., my troops held virtually the same position, changes only having been made to induce attack upon us, or by threatening attack, to keep the enemy from going against Gen. Pope. In this I was successful.

As Gen. McDowell's order to me at that time alone prevented an immediate engagement of my troops, and resulted in prolonging the "inaction" which you condemn in me, I deem it proper to state these facts fully.

I was a witness before the court of inquiry relative to Gen. McDowell's conduct, which was in session at the same time and in the same building with my court; but was prohibited from giving this statement in full and explaining "wherein my statement differed from his testimony before my court." Gen. McDowell was informed by the court that, though I could not make this explanation without a change of his question, he should have liberty to change his question to bring out the facts. This he declined to do and my mouth was consequently closed.

It is true Gen. McDowell testified to a "want of memory" of any such verbal order sent to me—and had himself endorsed only by the testimony of an officer, who was presented to the court as a witness against me, though a *member of that same court in which he was sitting judicially!* whose testimony was that he was not present when such an order was given.

Against Gen. McDowell's want of recollection and the endorsement it had, I produced the positive testimony of my chief of staff, who brought me McDowell's *renewed* order; and I am now prepared to verify his testimony by additional and conclusive evidence.

I have shown that my "inaction" up to the afternoon of the 29th was in strict obedience of orders.

I now meet your charge of "inaction" up to a later hour on that day.

After Gen. McDowell left me (early afternoon, 29th) and up to the time of Gen. Pope's positive order of 4.30 P. M. (29th) reaching me, 6:30 P. M., I was certainly as free to exercise my "discretion" under Pope's "joint order" as McDowell was. Under the "joint order" he elected to divide our forces and march to another field, where it seems he arrived too late for his troops to be successfully used. Under it I elected to hold my position, neutralize double my force, and, in the enemy's opinion, saved, by my action, both Pope and McDowell from "capture or total route." I submit to you, sir, if I can prove all this, as I can, whether my conduct "within a short distance of the field of battle under the sound of our guns," and *without* "an order to go into the fight," was not *most* advantageous to our army and the country.

It is now proper to introduce the subject of the new evidence I am ready to produce on these points, and which is indicated in the letters of Generals Longstreet, Wilcox and others. The orders of General Pope on the 29th were *based* upon the supposition that the "whole force of the enemy" was still some distance from the field and would not arrive within thirty to fifty hours, *i. e.* "by to-morrow night or the next day." This basis of the order was, to my knowledge and that of Gen. McDowell, untrue. I had come in contact with the enemy and was coming into position when the order was received. I knew that Longstreet had arrived, and I was convinced, from information in my possession, that the remainder of the enemy's main forces must be near the field, and observation satisfied me they were arriving.

The letters above referred to, state that Longstreet's command commenced arriving on the field at 9 A. M., 29th—about the hour Pope's order was penned—that he was ready to receive any attack after 11, and that he was particularly anxious to bring on the battle after 12 M.

This additional evidence also shows, as I claimed at the time, that an attack at any time after 12 M., by my corps alone, must have resulted disastrously, and that the mere fact of my presence on the Gainesville road kept a largely superior force of

2

the enemy in my front, and diverted them from supporting Jackson and overwhelming Pope.

I am not calling in question the propriety of Gen. McDowell's movements of the 29th. I am merely sustaining my views of the case as claimed at the time, and I ask you, sir, is it not now demonstrated beyond doubt that the very order which McDowell could not recollect, "to remain where I was"—was the one of all others for him to give. There can be no dispute among military men on this point.

To show that my views are in no wise changed and that I now raise no new issue, I quote from my defence before the court.

"I come now to say a few words of the testimony of General McDowell. I "shall speak of him as a witness with entire calmness and candor, because, "though I speak with regret, I shall speak with no disrespect. His testi- "mony, taken as a whole, has astonished me beyond measure. I feel that it "has done me more harm and more wrong—I charitably hope unintentional "wrong—than has been done to me by all the rest of the testimony of the "prosecution put together."

"It is well that this alleged order, 'to put my troops in there,' to me by "General McDowell does not so appear charged as specified, for now I will "demonstrate that he did not then give me, and cannot be believed to have "given me, any such order." * * * "It would have been proclaimed forth- "with at the head quarters of General Pope; it would have been blazoned among "these charges and specifications side by side with the order itself, and, if true, "it ought to have made the words of exculpation which General Pope uttered to "me at Fairfax Court House on the 2d September, four days afterwards, choke "him as he spoke. But it is not true that General McDowell then, or at any "time on that day, gave me any such order 'to put my troops in there.' or to "do anything of the kind; and fortunate is it for General McDowell that it is "not true, for if he had given me any such mandate to thrust my corps in over "that broken ground between Jackson's right and the separate enemy massing "in my front, the danger and disaster of such a movement would have been "then and now upon his hands. I am glad that I can say that Gen. McDowell "is utterly in error upon this point, and is no way chargeable with such fatal "military blunder. It is not alone that I am as clear as I can be as to any "fact in my life that I received at that time no such order from him, but it is "demonstrated in what I have said, as well as in what else stands proved in "this record, that no such order to me could have been then by him given.

"Unable, as he testifies, by habit of mind accurately to remember the divi- "sions of time, he has plainly confused in his testimony, * * * "the situations, the sayings, and the doings of different days. I have said "that I would speak of his testimony with calmness and candor, and without "disrespect. Under strong provocations I have kept my word, but I have "demolished his testimony before you, and with it the whole prosecution falls, "and the accusation is left to the condemnation and derision of all just men."

This narrative covers the period of time between noon of the 29th and the hour of receipt of Pope's order of 4:30 P. M.

You repeat Gen. Pope's main charge: that I failed to make,

under his order of 4:30 P. M., August 29, an attack which would have caused " *the defeat and capture of Jackson's army.*"

That order was:—

"HEADQUARTERS IN THE FIELD,
"*August* 29, 1862—4.30 *P. M.*

"Your line of march brings you in on the enemy's right flank. I desire you "to push forward into action at once on the enemy's flank, and, if possible, "on his rear, keeping your right in communication with Gen. Reynolds. The "enemy is massed in the woods in front of us, but can be shelled out as soon "as you engage their flank. Keep heavy reserves, and use your batteries, "keeping well closed to your right all the time. In case you are obliged to fall "back, do so to your right and rear, so as to keep in close communication with "the right wing.

"JOHN POPE,
"*Major General Commanding.*"

The evidence given on the trial shows very clearly that this order was not delivered to me until about 6:30 P. M., about sunset; that the orders to carry it into execution were at once given by me and attended to in person; that the preparations could not be completed in season to make the attack before dark, and that the nature of the ground was such as to make a night attack impracticable. My witnesses as to the hour of the receipt of the order (about 6:30) were Gen. Sykes, Col. Locke, Capt. Montieth and Lieutenants Weld and Ingham. Against these officers, then as now widely known and respected, Gen. Pope was able to introduce only the testimony of his relative who brought the order, and the orderly who came with him. On the receipt of this order, I gave, as was my duty, *a written acknowledgment* to the officer bearing it. He verifies this fact, and yet Gen. Pope, when called upon in court to produce it and thus establish the vital point of the time of his order reaching me, *could not find it.* So also of several other letters of importance against him and in my favor.

When Gen. Pope made this charge, to put on me the blame of his defeat, he little thought I should ever have the proofs I now have, and which he and others now labor so hard to exclude from the case. He has made many vain boasts; but none more wild and extravagant, with less of truth and sense than *this* charge made against me, which he attempts, now as then, to sustain only by such reckless assertions as the following:

"I believe, in fact, I am positive, that at 5 o'clock in the afternoon of the "29th, Gen. Porter had in his front, no considerable body of the enemy;

"I believed then, as I am very sure now, that it was easily practicable for him "to have turned the right flank of Jackson and to have fallen upon his rear; "that if he had done so, we should have gained a decisive victory over the "army under Jackson *before he could have been joined by any of the forces of "Longstreet;* and that the army of Gen. Lee would have been so crippled and "checked by the destruction of this large force as to have been no longer in "condition to prosecute further operations of an aggressive character."

On this "emphatic opinion," says Judge Advocate-General Holt, "coincided in by McDowell and Roberts," I was condemned.

McDowell, under the same theory in regard to the commander and strength of the enemy fronting me, testifies if I had attacked the right wing of the enemy (Jackson) on the 29th, the result would "have been decisive in our favor."

Though I then knew it I had not other witnesses than myself to prove that it was not Jackson's isolated corps alone before us, but Lee's whole army; and that for me to have attacked Jackson's flank was impossible, as Lee's whole army lay between Jackson and me and would probably have led to Pope's capture, not possibly to Jackson's—to our total rout, not to the enemy's defeat.

To prove this, new testimony is now attainable, and on this I am entitled to a new hearing.

My opinions then (29th) were the same as they are now—and I quote once more from my defence pointing to the fact:

"If the major general, late commanding the army of Virginia, whose in-"spector general is, at least, my nominal prosecutor here, doubts the truth of "what I now say, let him produce, if he can, as I asked him to produce at the "trial, the note which I sent him by Captain Douglass Pope, at dusk, in reply "to his order of 4.30 P. M., of the 27th, directing me to attack Jackson's right, "and he will then learn, or at least recollect, what I at that moment judged "concerning both the position of the enemy and my own. Let him publish "that note, since it has not been produced, if he can, even at this late day, find "it, and then all who choose to compare that note with what I have just stated, "will know that the military theory of the position which I now express with "all confidence has ever since that day remained in my mind unchanged."

The next day gave sad proof in my justification—though the prosecution managed to exclude the evidence from the trial, and that alone would be ground for a new trial. The facts are these: on that day—the 30th August—Pope withdrew me from before Longstreet, collected all his force on Jackson, attacked, and was defeated. My corps fought well, and suffered great loss. In Jackson's report to Lee he speaks of our attack; of the "fierce and sanguinary struggle;" the "fury of the assault;" the "impetuous and well sustained onsets." But Pope being again defeated, again blames me and my corps. In his *report* he says: "the attack of Porter was neither vigorous nor persistent; and his troops soon retired in considerable confusion." The charge sent to the court martial imputes to me, "slowness"—"falling back"—"drawing away"—and "not making the resistance demanded by his position." I was not *allowed* to acquit myself, and convict him. *For when the trial came on, the prosecution withdrew the charge*, and prevailed with the court, over my earnest protest, to admit no evidence of the facts on that day, to explain the transactions and prove the situation of the day before. It was a cunning and most unfair proceeding, and a false technical quibble to shut out my most material proof, and now Pope denies that Jackson's report refers to me, and my men. He says, "Porter is deceived." I say I am not deceived; and that he does not speak the truth. I challenge the proof before any honest tribunal.

The situation on both days was simply this. It was now the crisis of the campaign. Pope's "fooling" had all failed. The "stories" he put out—which you think so skillful—had not "fooled" the rebels. They knew the truth—preferring to get it elsewhere—and had come with a superior force to give him battle. The stratagem they practiced had no foolery in it. It was the old maxim of war, "*take position when you can, and induce the attack;*" skilful tactics, which the book of regulations for our army thus expounds, in the chapter on battles: "to be safe in making the attack, requires a larger force than "the enemy, or better troops and favorable ground;" and, "when the artillery can be well posted, and advantage of "ground secured, await the enemy and compel him to attack." Pope's braggart temper and utter want of military penetration let him fall into the trap, and he made the unfortunate attacks the enemy wanted him to make. Here is his own account. On the 30th of August at 5:30 A. M. he telegraphed Halleck of the battle of the 29th, "we have fought a terrific battle; "the enemy was driven from the field; we have lost "8,000 men. From the appearance of the field, the en-"emy has lost at least two to one. He stood strictly on "the defensive, and every assault was made by us." Jackson reported that "every advance was most successfully driven "back." Of the next day's battle, Pope says, "I advanced "to the attack as rapidly as I was able to bring my forces into "action." To his army, he said, "*you will pursue the enemy "in his retreat, and press him vigorously all the day.*" Every one knows the deplorable result, and such were the tactics that led to it. But Pope never wants facts and reasons to excuse himself. He generally has a variety, and no two hold together. In this case he has an assortment.

In his report, dated January 27, 1863, he says, "at no time "could I have fought a successful battle with the immensely superior force of the enemy which confronted me, and which was "able, at any time, to outflank me and bear my small army to "the dust."

To the *court martial* he declared that if I had not failed him, he would have "defeated and captured Jackson's army on the 29th, and have beaten and destroyed Longstreet and Lee in detail as they came up afterwards." The truth is Lee and Longstreet were with Jackson already, and of this we now have the fullest proof.

If this seems to you to be going somewhat into Pope's history I desire you to consider that it adheres strictly to the charge against me, and my proper and true defence to it; and it has the most direct bearing on the case to add, that if Pope believed the charges, if he had any honest belief or reasonable suspicion of their truth—that "I failed him," and caused his defeat and the escape of his enemy—it was *his* duty to prefer the charges not that of his Inspector General. In that case I could only be tried by a court detailed by the President. The law says when the general who commands, &c., "shall be the accuser or prosecutor," the court shall be detailed by the President. Pope was surely the accuser. He brought the accusation in his official report. A military commission was first ordered on *his* charges. He was the principal witness for the prosecution. He testified to the committee on the conduct of the war, that *he* "brought me to justice." Then surely a trial, in which his part as accuser was disavowed, and the charges got up were signed by his staff officer Gen. Benjamin S. Roberts, was a fraud on me and on the law, tainting the proceeding that grew out of it, and which vitiates and annuls it.

On that ground, too, I am entitled to a new hearing.

You, sir, may ask why now, I have to offer so much new evidence which should have been attainable at the time from our own ranks ?

I reply that it was not obtainable, for the following reasons :—

1st. That, the times and circumstances checked a free expression or offering of testimony.

2d. That permission was refused me by the Secretary of War, early in the trial, to send my aids to the army at Fredericksburg, to see witnesses and gather testimony.

3d. That when I did send, on my own responsibility, my aids to the army, letters to and from them and others, were purloined or opened and robbed of information.

4th. Some witnesses I was persuaded could furnish reliable information in my favor, but of their names and location I was not apprised and others, whom I knew would testify to very important facts in my behalf, did not appear till the moment they were called to testify.

In the former case I, of course, lost not only the benefit of their testimony but also the benefit of the information they had as to what other persons could prove in my favor. In the latter case I was compelled to produce witnesses without knowing myself, or my counsel knowing, what particular facts they were possessed of and how to elicit them fully. These witnesses, whose names I had, were all given at the opening of the court on the demand of Judge-Advocate Holt and on his assurance that he would secure their early attendance.

Of these irregularities I complained to the court, and to the government. They give additional grounds for a rehearing.

You have been misled enough against me, to believe and repeat what Pope says. To my offer of proof of the enemy's strength in numbers and position, he objects—*that I had nothing to do with it. I was ordered to attack. It was my duty to attack if I lost every man I had, and no matter whether the enemy was* 20,000 *or* 100,000.

To understand whether the strength and position of the enemy (not of Jackson's force) was competent evidence for me to produce in reply to a charge—the charge must be known. It was this: That I was ordered to attack *Jackson's* flank, that I disobeyed and thus prevented the defeat and capture of Jackson's army. My offer is to prove that Jackson's flank was not where Pope thought it was, nor where my force could reach it; that another force than Jackson's, more than double my numbers, was posted in strong position between me and Jackson, and if I had attacked it, I would have ensured my own defeat and capture and that, probably, of Pope's whole army—that I knew this at the time—that I knew it at the trial but could not prove it—but can prove it now.

Referring to me you say "what *business was it to him* whether he was cut to pieces or not?" Often it may be no business to an officer whether he is cut to pieces or not. But when he is ordered to fall on the flank of one corps of the enemy, in order to insure *its* defeat or capture, and he cannot fall on it and defeat and capture it—it is his business, not to be cut to pieces in falling on another much larger body of the enemy which he was not ordered to attack, and which if he did attack, must have defeated and captured him, and the army of the general giving the order. Do I not prove I am not guilty, *in not doing what I should not and could not have done.* Surely I sweep away by such proof every atom of the charge, as you will see if you study it, and *leave nothing for the sentence to stand on.*

You quote "as true facts in the case," the assertion of Lee's Engineer-in-Chief (who is he?) that Longstreet's command was not on the field until the morning of the 30th August, the day *after* I was confronted by his whole force—when Longstreet's own letter to sustain my assertion of his presence on the 29th was lying on your desk at the time you made it I must suppose this fact, as useful to me as it is damaging to Gen. Pope, was unintentionally overlooked by you.

My conviction and sentence were based, it is assumed, upon the evidence produced before the court, but the public importance of the conviction and the vindication of the magnitude of the sentence were based largely upon the supposed infinite damage my conduct had occasioned. How largely the court was influenced by these *as sumptions* I need only refer to Mr. Holt's review.

All just men will agree that it will not do to use and laud "rebel testimony" against me—as in the quotations from Gen.

J. E. B. Stuart—while the carefully considered and particularly stated evidence in my favor made by Generals Longstreet, Wilcox and others, is discarded.

The report of Stuart to his commander of dragging bushes to deceive our troops is true no doubt; but the evidence is within your reach to-day, was, when you spoke in the Senate, that the whole of Longstreet's corps of 27,000 men, was also in front of my command of less than 11,000 men.

You dwell on my "animus." So did Judge-Advocate Holt, and it was his chief *argument* to prove the alleged *facts!* He meant that I was ill-disposed to Gen. Pope and well-disposed to Gen. McClellan, and *wished* to see Pope fail and McClellan put in command. That animus, or state of mind—to convict me of acts and deeds—he tries to show from certain selected telegrams I sent to certain officers. Do you know that those officers—as zealous patriots as breathe—saw nothing in them wrong, no disaffection, no spirit of disobedience, only an anxious concern for the publie interest, and an anxious distrust of Pope's capacity to command the army. Do you know their accuracy was verified? Do you know that Mr. Lincoln thanked me warmly for those very telegrams? If they are evidence in the case it is evidence in my favor; and surely the argument of bad *motive* is silenced, when I disprove every alleged *fact.*

When I am heard—as I shall be sooner or later—I shall show, by original despatches written by me on the field to officers of my corps, that I directed the execution of Gen. Pope's orders with promptness and vigor. Most of these despatches have come into my possession since the trial; they will be substantiated as originals, by officers of high rank and position who received them. They will close the mouths of honest men against my alleged "animus" toward Gen. Pope.

The final point of your speech is as follows:

"There is one other point to which I wish to allude. During "this very trial, during the very pendency of the trial, Fitz "John Porter said in the presence of my informant, who is a "man that most of you know, and who is to-day in the em- "ployment of Congress, and whose word I would take as soon "as I would most men's—though I told him I would not use "his name, but I will give his sworn testimony, taken down "within two minutes after the utterance was made—Fitz John "Porter said in his presence 'I was not true to Pope, and "there's no use in denying it.'"

To me, such evidence seems scarcely worthy of notice—for the person that makes a statement, which, if true, is so damning in its character, and then begs the concealment of his name, is not worthy of recognition by men. That as presented by you it had any effect upon the minds of Senators, I cannot conceive—many of them being lawyers, who know that such evidence would not be admitted before any tribunal. My reply to you, sir, is that the statement by whomsoever made and however testified to, is FALSE in every particular. Aside from my general character for reticence when in the army, I certainly had no inducement to lose my senses pending my trial, and falsely assert in any one's presence just what General Pope was forty-five days endeavoring to prove. Where was this reliable witness then? Why did he not then and there testify to my confessed guilt? What restrained him for all these years, and why does he now recollect or produce evidence, which, if credible, would long ago have ended my appeal? I am ashamed to offer, to be compelled to offer an argument against assertions so palpably contrived and so wholly unsustained by probabilities—so wholly at variance with my whole life and conduct.

You say that after a careful investigation for forty-five days, the court *unanimously* rendered a verdict against me. This may have been so, but you cannot know it unless some member has violated his oath "not to discover or disclose that vote unless required to give evidence thereof, (which has not been done) before a court of justice, in due course of law." But if true, the question is not what the court did decide, but what would be now decided with the new evidence I have to present—and you must know that the decision of that court does not affect the justice of my demand that the new evidence shall be heard in my defence.

And let me here say, that on my first appeal to the President, Gen. Grant (then at the head of the army) said to me what all fair men will endorse, that if I could prove what I asserted, and what my papers indicated, justice required the re-examination, and every member of my court should be glad of an opportunity to join in my appeal.

I have made my appeal to the President anew, and now await his action as to the appointment of a board of officers to investigate my case with all the *new* testimony adduceable. What I ask requires no opinion from the Administration as to the propriety or injustice of my conviction.

I simply ask to be heard.

Plain and honest minds will look with suspicion upon opposition to such a request, especially when the request is made by one whose life has been spent as an officer in the service of the Government and whose record will not suffer by contrast with any of his accusers. Plain and honest people will enquire—do now enquire—why such violent opposition to my being heard and to the hearing of *all* the testimony? If, as is asserted, the re-opening of the case, will only deepen the public conviction of the justice of my punishment, why should my enemies, and they alone, oppose it? You know that a divided public opinion as to the justice of my conviction is not what Gen. Pope and others would like. Why not, then, seize upon this opportunity, if Gen. Pope has so clear a case, and fix and fasten the stigma forever? Is it not due to the "truth of history" that the justice of my condemnation should be made so palpable, that the scores of our most patriotic and most learned men with more than half of our leading and influential journals will cease their advocacy of my case?

Is it not due to Gen. Pope and "the truth of history" that so admirable an opportunity as my re-hearing would present, should be made available to show what *his* real business in life was at the time of his Virginia campaign.

You think that he was sorely misunderstood by the country at that time and has been since; and you re-assert that but for me—but for my treasonable conduct—his campaign, that, as you state it, had for its mission the relief of McClellan, by some fighting, and a good deal of "fooling," would have ended in the capture of Jackson, the destruction of Longstreet and the end of the war;—surely, if all this glory was lost to Gen. Pope by my conduct, is it just to him to withold the facts from an incredulous public?

Neither Gen. Pope or others can longer take refuge behind the "want of power" to re-open my case—the "bad precedent" it would fix upon the army and the like. The power has been found and exercised—the precedent has been fixed and rightly too—and to the public view Gen. Pope and all others who oppose my simple request "to be heard before a tribunal known to be impartial," stand, and ever will stand with the suspicion fixed upon them that they shun the re-examination because they dare not meet the TRUTH.

I have endeavored to refer to the main points of your speech against me, and, though measurably restricted in my reply, I make it with unabated faith in the ultimate justice of my Government—long delayed as it has been—longer delayed as it may be.

Sustained as I am by hosts of friends, whose hands I have never grasped, but whose hearts and words and pens are active in my behalf—sustained by the old and true and tried friends who have not turned upon me in adversity—but best sustained by my ever-present and never-failing faith that a just and generous people will not permit my wrongs to go un-redressed, I shall go on to the end, obtaining my justification from the government who owes it to me, or leaving it, if GOD wills it, a legacy for my children to demand and obtain.

Respectfully,

FITZ JOHN PORTER.

www.ingramcontent.com/pod-product-compliance
Lightning Source LLC
LaVergne TN
LVHW011146110826
845150LV00008B/2541

* 9 7 8 1 4 1 8 1 9 2 1 4 3 *